You Wonder,  I Wonder,  He wonders,  She  Wonders

Paul  Duchateau
James Pierpont

AFREE PUBLISHING WEBSITE AT Montgomery Hill

$$f\_xj \;-\!- \; d/d\text{-}x \; (f\_xj) = 0$$

$$j = 1.\,2.\,3. \;\dots\text{..}n$$

-----Akira Takayama

Calculus of Serval Variables

---- E. K. Mclachlan

$P(z) \; --- \; Z^{\wedge}(-2) \; = Q(z)$

$\text{Log}(1+2) \; = \; z - \tfrac{1}{2}\,(z^{\wedge}2) + 1/3\,(z^{\wedge}3) - 1/4\,(z^{\wedge}4) + \ldots.$

$\text{Log}\,(x^{\wedge}a) = a\,(\log x)$

--- A. Zygmand
--- Ken Wolf

Pastpel   (important  words)


Spiky colors
Rags in rainbow
pascal pattern
Intranet
Script
Scene
Cast
Drama
Scottish
Tornado
Typhoon
 Lodge
Resort

Elements of point set topology

--- john baurn

Introductory analysis

---- Richard bagby

A concrete approach to abstract algebra

-----w. w. sawyer

The calculus with  Analytic Geometry

---- Louise Leithold

Exponential Function

$E(x+y) = E(x)E(y)$

$E^{(x+y)} = E^x \times E^y$

$x, y$ in $R$

$E(0) = 1$

-----Richard Bagby

Longarithmic  Function


If    T:   (0, infinity)  >>>   R such That


T(x, y) = T(x) + T(y)

Log(xy) = log(x) + log(y)




ps:  T(x/y) = T(x) –T(y)


*      T(1)=0

- log(x) = integral _(1, x)  1/j dj,   j ranges from 1 to x,

- Log (x)  derivative = 1/x,     (x>0)

Nice algebra to think about


$P^2 = 1$

|
V

$P^2 - 1 = 0$

|
V

$(p+1)(p-1) = 0$

|
V
$p+1=0$, or $p-1=0$

|
V

$P = -1$. $P = 1$


----- W. W Sawyer

Problems and solutions in ordinary differential equations

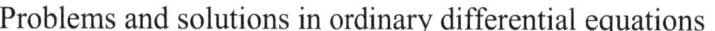

----- Fred Brauer

----- John A. Nohel

$$\| q-u \| \ == \ \text{Root} \left( \text{integral} \ \_(c, d) \ [q(t) - u(t)]^2 \ (w(t) dt \right.$$

$$|x| = \begin{cases} -x, & \text{if } x < 0 \\ x, & \text{if } x \geq 0 \end{cases}$$

$$\sqrt{x^2} = |x|$$

Infant words


Cute
Camping
Laundry
Vent
Pot
Dresser
Base board
Hearboard
Trees
Foot
Leg
Mouth
Outdoor
Siren
Hum
Food
Sleep
Laugh

Purity


Trip
Tip
Rip
Put
Its
Ally
Pity
Slove
Vet
Vest
Column
Dutch
Break
Bike
Coke

Use the method of successive substitutions to apprimate:

A solution to a funny equation

Solve for x, if    $x = x/2 + 1/x$

Minus x/2 on both sides

$x - x/2 = x/2 + 1/x - x/2$

$x/2 = 1/x$

,ultiple 2x on both sides

$2x (x/2) = 2x(1/x)$

$X^2 == 2$

Take roots on both sides

$x =$ root 2,  $x = -$ root2

Ux - Uxxxxx - F (x, t, u, ux, uxx, uxxx)


Intergrable fifth order kdv type equation




--- Juan ming yuan
--- Jiahong Wu

Linear algebra with application

----Jeanne Agnew
--- Robert Knapp

Journal Literature of the physical sciences

--- alice, lefler, prinacle

# Fundamental concepts of arithmetic

---- Sidney hacker
---- Wilfred Barnes
---- Calvin Long

If a matrix B is mxm,  the homogeneous system

Bt=0  has a non-trivial solution if anf only if    det(B)=0

----Craig Barch

What is X^tB X when   B = [ 1, 3, /  3, 2 ],   x in R^2

By definition, we know

X^t B X  = [x1, x2] [ 1 3 / 3 2 ] [x1 /x2]

= [ x1 +3x2  /  3x1 +2x2] ^T   [x1 x2]

= (x1 +3x2) (x1) + (3x1 +2x2) (x2)

= x1^2 + 3 x1 x2 +3 x1 x2+2xz^2
X1^2 +  6x1 x2 +2x2 ^2

------ Phyllis Niklas

Interesting matrix

Definition, A is symmetric if and only if A transpose = A

Or $A^t = A$

If a is 3 by 3, then a13 = a31, a23 = a32

Definition, A is diagonal means, a ij=0, i-j > 0 or i-j<0

A = [ 1 0 / 0 2 ] is diagonal

-----Jamie Brooks

Euclidean Algorithm


Greatest common divisor

$d = \text{GCD} = (m, n)$


example    $(48510, 1197) = 63$


$(824670, 20349) = 1071$

Interesting  inequality


If t >0,  a <b, then   at <  bt

And  t+a  = t +b




---- Carole Sloan
----Ardith Ericson
----Jim McPherson

An introduction to linear algebra

---Hans  Samelson

Elementary numberical  analysis

---- kendall Atkinson

Let P be a matrix , and p is 2x2,   order of (p) =2,

P= (a11, a12 / a21, a22),

Det (p) =  a11 a22 -  a12 a21

If det(p)  =0,  then p is singalar,
otherwise, det(p) non zero, p is non-singular

---- Donovan Shuang

Complex varibles

---- Murray r. Spiegel

Lim n→infinity $(1 + z/n) = 1$

If all z as real number

In other words, $|1 + z/n -1| < e$

For all $e > 0$, $n > N = |z|/e$

Rouche's Theorem

If $p(j)$ and $h(j)$ are analytic inside, and on a simple closed curve D, and if

$|h(j)| < |p(j)|$, then

$P(j) + h(j)$ and $p(j)$ have the same zeros inside D

Gauss's Mean value theorem

If A(t) is analytic inside and on a circle B with center at 0,
Radius n, then A(t) is the mean of the values of A(t) on B,

I, e,

$$A(0) = \frac{1}{2\pi} \int_0^{2\pi} A(0 + n e^{is}) \, ds$$

Sevess elles


To take a comment
We must do algebra
A factor is hidden
A variable is chosen


A tennis court
Balls fly high
With a perfect catch
A smell climbs to mt fuji

More wonder

Why computer matters?
Why do numbers count?
Do you care less your paperwork?
Yes, computer is one way to improve life quality

---thomas tymoczko (1992)

Taylor series at x=m

$$P(x) = P(m) + p'(m)(x-m) + (x-m)^2 q(x)$$

p, q polynomials

---- Kathy Buxie

Gilbert and Page-Brinsome
--humor on derivatives


When I was small
I used to break a rule
I often do multiplication by mind
I always enjoy division of any kind


A child grows
She assumes dreams
A dream comes true
She knows product and quotient rule

Product and quotient rule   j. p. morgan

$(pq)' = p'q + pq'$

$(p/q)' = (p'q - pq') / q^2$

q is non zero
p q is differential functions

Topics in the theory of functions of one complex variables

---- w. H. J. Fuchs

Analysis

volume one

---- einar hille

Continuity

----g. b. Thomas

Experimental nuclear physics

---------- k. n. mikhin

Max (a, b) = sum of a, b /2 + |a-b|/2

Min (a, b) = sum of a, b /2 - |a-b|/2

c+d = max (a,b)
c-d = min (a, b)

----george thomas

Innumeracy


---john allen paulos

What is mathematics?

----ian stewart
---richard courant
---herbert robbins

Theorem

Suppose that

$|f(x, y) - L| <= g(x, y)$
For all $(x, y)$ in the interior of some circle centered ay $(xo, yo)$, except possibly at $(xo, yo)$, then

if $\text{Lim } g(x, y) = 0$, $(x, y) \dashrightarrow (xo, yo)$

then $\text{Lim } |f(x, y) - L| = 0$

or $\text{Lim } (x, y) \rightarrow (xo, yo) \ f(x, y) = L$

---robert smith
---roland b. minton

Mathematical Logic

----W. V. Quine

f'(t) = zf(t)

---- R. C. Maclamy
----V. J. Mizel

½ + 1/3 + 1/3 =1

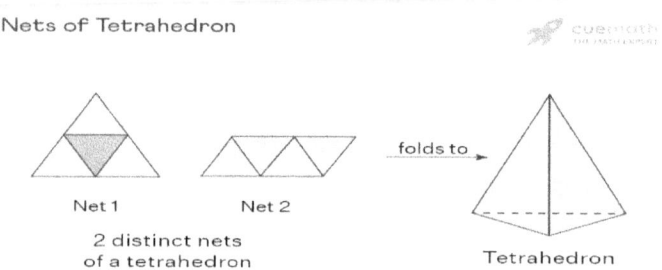

Nets of Tetrahedron

Net 1    Net 2

folds to

2 distinct nets
of a tetrahedron

Tetrahedron

Tetrahedram,  a trianglers meeting 3 of a point…

-----Lawrence Brenton

Some applications of mechanics to mathematics

---- V. A. Uspenskii
----Ian Sneddon
----Halina Moss

Amazing math

½ + 1/3 + ¼ - 1/12 = 1

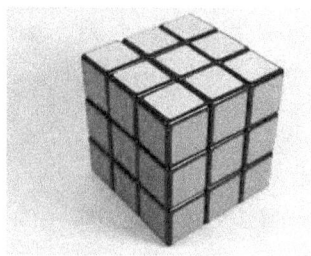

Cube,  squares meeting 3 at a point

---ana vasiliu

Way to go, math is nice

½ +1/4 +1/3 – 1/12 =1

Octahedron: triangles meeting 4 at a point

----Seth Isis
---Osiris Rhind

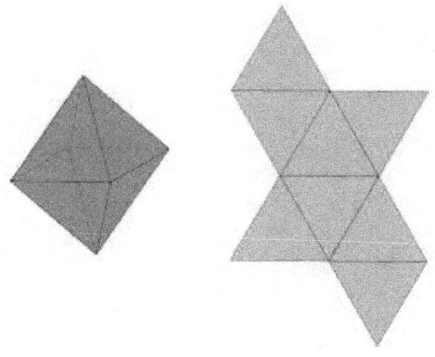

Tammie and  Wilson math

½ + 1/3 + 1/5 − 1/30 =1

Dodecahedron: a pentagons meeting 3 at a point

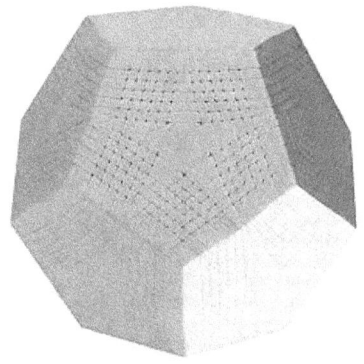

6 = 3+2+1

----- enclid, Fermat, Mersenne,

College Algebra

-----Jimmie Gilbert
----James Spencer
----Linda  Gilbert

John De Pillis's math humor

Paul ritger is a three year old
Young and restless, also bold,
He adds zero to prime numbers,
He divides those by five
He ends up archilling odds
A mixed solution, full grins of members

Word twisters   --lewis Carroll

"contrariwise"  said
Tweedledeerson,   " if you agree,
In case you believe so, and
Have faith, it would be false
If your home is in new York, while
Your job is in seattle, so you're not
Sure where you were, and it is sweet
That you are somewhere which is an odd logic"

Proof
Promote
Young
Bone
Fish
Hamster
Kibble
Look
Junemark

4! / root 4  ==  (4x3x2x1) /2 = 12

**loxodrome**

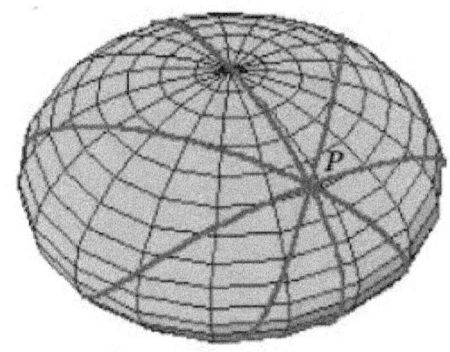

A Loxodrome

-----murray schechter
-----allentown, pa

A fresh method of trisection


An owl with whitehair
And taxi in air, in speedy speed
Telescoped to a cloud forrest
The bird is a feather to think
We see flights on a screen
We check mark a boeing 777 to rent




-----laura welch
----dave brooks
----alan bush

www.ingramcontent.com/pod-product-compliance
Lightning Source LLC
Chambersburg PA
CBHW081222170526
45165CB00009B/2916

* 9 7 8 1 3 8 7 8 5 0 6 6 2 *